INVASION ALERT!

INVASION OF THE ZEBRA MUSSELS

DEVON PATRICK

Enslow PUBLISHING

Please visit our website, www.enslow.com. For a free color catalog of all our high-quality books,
call toll free 1-800-398-2504 or fax 1-877-980-4454

Published in 2027 by
Enslow Publishing
2544 Clinton Street
Buffalo, NY 14224

Portions of this work were originally authored by Michael Rajczak and published as *Animal Invaders: Destroying Native Habitats: Attack of the Zebra Mussels*. All new material in this edition is authored by Devon Patrick.

Cataloging-in-Publication Data
Names: Patrick, Devon.
Title: Invasion of the zebra mussels / Devon Patrick.
Description: Buffalo, NY : Enslow Publishing, 2027. | Series: Invasion alert! | Includes glossary and index.
Identifiers: ISBN 9781978548459 (pbk.) | ISBN 9781978548466 (library bound) | ISBN 9781978548473 (ebook)
Subjects: LCSH: Zebra mussel--Juvenile literature. | Introduced mollusks--Juvenile literature.
Classification: LCC QL430.7.D8 D486 2027 | DDC 594.4--dc23

Printed in China

Photos Credits: Cover, p. 1 Brendan Goff/Shutterstock.com; cover, p. 1, 3, 4, 6, 8, 10, 12, 14, 16, 18, 20, 22, 23, 24 (dot pattern) Nurin Nabila A/Shutterstock.com; p. 4, 6, 8, 10, 12, 14, 16, 18, 20 (sidebar frame) HST6/Shutterstock.com; p. 5, 11 Stukel, Sam - USFWS; p. 7 Vitalii Hulai/Shutterstock.com; p. 9 Jeff Caughey/Shutterstock.com; p. 9 Peter Hermes Furian/Shutterstock.com; p. 13 Paul Reeves Photography/Shutterstock.com; p. 15 ChWeiss/Shutterstock.com; p. 17 Carismarkus.ch/Shutterstock.com; p. 19 Alyh M/Shutterstock.com; p. 21 Brittany McKenney/Shutterstock.com

CPSIA compliance information: Batch #QSENS27: For further information, contact Enslow Publishing, New York, New York, at 1-800-398-2504.

CONTENTS

Words in the glossary appear in **bold** type the first time they are used in the text.

A BOAT JOURNEY

Zebra mussels are small shellfish. They're native to, or originally from, the Caspian Sea and Black Sea between Europe and Asia. But in the late 1980s, these freshwater critters **invaded** the Great Lakes of the United States! This **invasive species** can be harmful to native animals and plants when put into a new **habitat**. It's difficult—or impossible—to stop their spread.

It's believed zebra mussel **larvae** arrived in the **ballast** water of ships that traveled here with goods from Europe. They've been causing problems ever since.

STAY ALERT

The Great Lakes water system contains about 20 percent of all of Earth's surface fresh water. It provides drinking water for over 40 million people in the U.S. and Canada.

Boats that are left in the water for a long period of time can become coated with zebra mussels. They are very difficult to clean off!

WHAT ARE ZEBRA MUSSELS?

Zebra mussels are bivalves, which means they have two shells. These shells may be rounded or "D" shaped, with a soft body inside. The bottom shell is flat so that it can lie against a hard surface. The top shell is more curved. The top shell is held to the bottom shell by a **hinge** that's somewhat flexible, or easy to bend.

Zebra mussels are small—only about the size of a fingernail. Their shells can be any shade of yellow or brown, from dark to light.

STAY ALERT

Mussels, clams, scallops, and oysters are all part of the mollusk family. Mollusks are animals that have soft bodies. Many are protected by hard shells.

Zebra mussels get their name from the striped pattern on their shells.

STICK TO IT!

Zebra mussels use threadlike strands to stick to hard surfaces, such as boats, rocks, and logs. These strands come out from underneath the bottom shell. When they arrived in the Great Lakes, zebra mussels made new homes on the flat surfaces of boats before anyone even knew they were there.

By sticking themselves to these boats, they traveled wherever the boats went. Zebra mussels quickly spread throughout the lakes and connected waterways. No one knew the zebra mussels were onboard until it was too late!

STAY ALERT

The zebra mussels that first landed in the Great Lakes found themselves in a **climate** just like what they were used to. They felt right at home!

Many boats accidentally transported zebra mussels all over the Great Lakes in the 1980s and 1990s.

MORE MUSSELS

Zebra mussels **reproduce** quickly. In the warm months, females release eggs into the water for fertilization. They can produce as many as one million eggs per year! With so many eggs, even a small group of zebra mussels can quickly turn into thousands.

Young zebra mussels, called larvae, have the tiny beginnings of their shells. As a larva's body and shells continue to grow, a hinge forms to connect the two shells on one side. Now, the zebra mussel must attach to a hard surface to survive.

STAY ALERT

Zebra mussels usually live three years, but some can live up to five.

Zebra mussel shells have a very sharp edge. Swimmers should wear water shoes or sneakers to keep their feet safe when zebra mussels are nearby.

TIME FOR LUNCH

Zebra mussels are **filter** feeders. They spend all day pumping water into their shells and over their gills. As the water passes over the gills, small bits of food are removed from the water, like algae, bacteria, and plankton. Zebra mussels can filter about 1 quart (0.95 L) of water a day, which means they eat a lot of plankton.

However, other native animals in freshwater lakes and rivers eat plankton as well. Zebra mussels are competing with them for food—and often winning!

STAY ALERT

Zebra mussels are one of more than 180 nonnative species now living in the Great Lakes. Others include carp, smelt, and sea lamprey.

Because zebra mussels are fairly new to the United States, they don't have many natural predators here. They are eaten by muskrats and some fish, but not enough to keep their populations under control.

UNWELCOME GUESTS

Zebra mussels need to stick to a hard surface in order to survive. They can attach to almost anything, including rocks, metal, wood, vinyl, glass, rubber, fiberglass, paper, plants, and even other mussels. The zebra mussels that make their homes inside pipes can cause major problems!

When pipes that bring water from lakes into towns get blocked, water can't get to businesses, schools, and even homes. Sometimes, zebra mussels can travel through pipes into homes. Blocked pipes can cost thousands of dollars to fix!

STAY ALERT

Zebra mussels move around to find a home by using a foot shaped like a tongue. They attach to a hard surface using threadlike fibers that grow from this foot.

Zebra mussels can even stick to other animals! Slow-moving creatures such as crayfish and turtles can have their entire body covered with zebra mussels.

OUT OF BALANCE

Lake Erie is one of the Great Lakes. It was once completely polluted. But once zebra mussels came and started filtering the water, it got much cleaner ... which caused problems too!

The water became so clear that sunlight could reach closer to the bottom of the lake. This increase in sunlight also increased the algae in the lake. Even though algae can be helpful, too much of it can be dangerous to wildlife. The entire **ecosystem** of the lake fell out of balance.

STAY ALERT

Lakes need a balance of plants and animals to stay healthy. When one species takes over, the whole ecosystem can be affected.

Some algae use up the oxygen in water, which fish need to live. Too little oxygen in the lake meant fish were dying. And some algae can even release poisons!

FIGHTING THE SPREAD

People are trying hard to fight back against the spread of zebra mussels. A Pennsylvania company created a coating that makes it hard for zebra mussels to attach to surfaces. Minnesota scientists are testing a deadly bacterium to see if it can kill zebra mussels without killing fish and plants. In Michigan, high-**pressure** water jets blast them off pipes. A business in California is training dogs to sniff out zebra mussels.

However, even with all these advancements, scientists think zebra mussels are likely here to stay!

STAY ALERT

Once zebra mussels are established in an area, it is very difficult to remove them. Preventing their spread is much more effective.

Since they arrived in the United States nearly 40 years ago, zebra mussels have continued to spread from the Great Lakes. They can be found as far away as California and Texas!

STOP THE ZEBRA MUSSELS!

It might be a long time, if ever, before scientists figure out a way to get rid of zebra mussels completely. But people can help slow their spread.

For example, fishermen should stop reusing bait that has been used in an area where zebra mussels live. Boat owners can help by keeping their boats clean. Before leaving a body of water, owners should check the boat and any equipment that touched the water. This will make sure that no zebra mussels spread to new areas!

STAY ALERT

Spread the word! Share what you've learned about zebra mussels and the trouble they can cause. Let's hope we can stop zebra mussels before they take over more waterways!

A Lake Michigan beach in Wisconsin is covered with millions of zebra mussel shells. Do your part to help stop this from happening to more beaches around the country!

GLOSSARY

ballast: heavy matter placed in a ship in such a way to help keep it steady and control the way it floats

climate: the average weather conditions of a place over a period of time

ecosystem: all the living things in an area

filter: to collect bits from a liquid passing through

habitat: the natural place where an animal or plant lives

hinge: a place where two things connect that allows them to open and close like a door

invade: to enter a place to take it over

invasive species: one kind of living thing likely to spread and be harmful when placed in a new area

larvae: the early stage of some animals, before they grow into adults

pressure: a force that pushes on something else

reproduce: to produce offspring

FACT CHECK

1. Zebra mussels are an invasive species in the __________.
   a. Caspian Sea b. Black Sea c. Great Lakes

2. Zebra mussels are named for the striped patterns on their __________.
   a. shells b. foot c. threadlike strands

3. Zebra mussels are filter feeders that eat lots of __________ each day.
   a. fish b. plankton c. mollusks

Answers: 1. c, 2. a, 3. b

ON THE INTERNET

Zebra Mussel Facts for Kids

https://kids.kiddle.co/Zebra_mussel

Learn all about zebra mussels, including where they come from and why they are considered invasive.

Student Page: Alien Invasion

plt.org/stuff/contentmgr/files/1/a10b723ca9ca5394ce34740e785ffa68/files/activity_12_student_pages.pdf

This brochure gives an overview of many kinds of invasive species.

Publisher's note to educators and parents: Our editors have carefully reviewed these websites to ensure that they are suitable for students. Many websites change frequently, however, and we cannot guarantee that a site's future contents will continue to meet our high standards of quality and educational value. Be advised that students should be closely supervised whenever they access the Internet.

INDEX